Unit 6

Weather for All Seasons

Mc
Graw
Hill
Education

Contents

Bob and Ben

Rob and Ben ran in.
Rob led Ben to the den.

Ben is on a big bed.
Bob can sit in the bin.

3

Bob is a little cat.
Ben can not fit with Bob.

Ben did not fit on it.
Bob did not like it.

Rob had Ben sit a lot.
Rob let Bob nap a lot.

Ben, Deb, Lin

Ben did a lot.
Ben let Cam hop in it.

Little Tom is a pet.
Dad let Tom sit.

Deb hit with the bat.
Deb ran a lap.

Ben had a red bib.
Ben bit the hot cob.

Lin bit the hot rib.
It is not bad, Lin!

Pack It Kim

Kim can kick a rock.
She can lick a pop.

Kim is hot on the dock!
Kim can go see Kit.

Kim can pack it.
It can sit on the rack.

Kit was on the deck.
Kim ran a lot.

Kim can pick ten.
Can Kit hit it?

Kick it, Nick!

Nick can not kick it.
Nick is a bit sad.

Nick can see Rick.
Rick can pack a sack.

Nick was on the dock.
Did Nick see it rock?

22

Nick can see Kim.
She can pick a fat bat.

Nick is back.

Nick can kick it a lot.

Ken was in bed.
Bob Cat was not.

Bob Cat is a pet.
Ken fed him a lot.

Mom did not like it dim.
She let Ken sit.

Do not sob my little Ken.
You are with Mom.

Ken sat on top.
Mom had to rock and rock.

Week 1 | Bob and Ben

DECODABLE WORDS
Target Phonics Elements
  Initial and Final Consonant *b*, Initial Consonant *l*; *b*: bed, Ben, bin, Bob, Rob; *l*: led, let, lot

HIGH-FREQUENCY WORDS
is, little
Review: a, and, like, the, to, with

Ben, Deb, Lin

DECODABLE WORDS
Target Phonics Elements
  Initial and Final Consonant *b*, Initial Consonant *l*; *b*: bat, Ben, bib, bit, cob, dab, Deb, rib; *l*: lap, led, let, Lin, lip, lot

HIGH-FREQUENCY WORDS
is, little
Review: a, the, with

Week 2 | Pack It Kim

DECODABLE WORDS
Target Phonics Elements
  Initial Consonant *k*, Final Digraph *ck*; *k*: kick, Kim, Kit; *ck*: deck, dock, kick, lick, pack, pick, rack, rock

HIGH-FREQUENCY WORDS
she, was
Review: a, go, is, see, the

Kick It, Nick!

DECODABLE WORDS
Target Phonics Elements
  Initial Consonant *k*, *Final Digraph ck*; *k*: kick, Kim; *ck*: back, dock, Nick, pack, pick, Rick, rock, sack

HIGH-FREQUENCY WORDS
she, was
Review: a, see, the

Week 3 | Rock Ken

DECODABLE WORDS
Target Phonics Elements
  Review Letters *h*: him; *e*: bed, fed, Ken, let, pet; *f*: fed; *r*: rock; *b*: bed, Bob, sob; *l*: let, lot; *k*: Ken; *ck*: rock

HIGH-FREQUENCY WORDS
are, is, little, my, she, was, with
Review: a, do, like, to, you

31

HIGH-FREQUENCY WORDS TAUGHT TO DATE
Grade K
a
and
are
can
do
go
he
I
is
like
little
my
see
she
the
to
was
we
with
you

DECODING SKILLS TAUGHT TO DATE
Initial and final consonant *m*; short *a*; initial *s*; initial and final consonant *p*; initial and final consonant *t*; initial and medial vowel *i*; initial and final consonant *n*; initial *c*; initial and medial vowel *o*; initial and final *d*; initial consonant *h*; initial and medial vowel *e*; initial consonants *f* and *r*; initial and final consonant *b*; initial consonant *l*; initial consonant *k*; final digraph *ck*